I0464012

SELLING IN YOUR TOWN

Your Guide to Running Your Small Business

DOUG MEYER

ARCHWAY
PUBLISHING

Archway Publishing books may be ordered through booksellers or by contacting:

Archway Publishing
1663 Liberty Drive
Bloomington, IN 47403
www.archwaypublishing.com
1 (888) 242-5904

Because of the dynamic nature of the Internet, any web addresses or
links contained in this book may have changed since publication and
may no longer be valid. The views expressed in this work are solely those
of the author and do not necessarily reflect the views of the publisher,
and the publisher hereby disclaims any responsibility for them.

Any people depicted in stock imagery provided by Thinkstock are models,
and such images are being used for illustrative purposes only.
Certain stock imagery © Thinkstock.

ISBN: 978-1-4808-3369-2 (sc)
ISBN: 978-1-4808-3370-8 (e)

Library of Congress Control Number: 2016910584

Print information available on the last page.

Archway Publishing rev. date: 8/12/2016

Doug Meyer purchased a local auto dealership in our community in 2013. Using common sense principles developed over his years in the retail and service industry Doug sparked new life into not only his auto dealership, but the whole city. His enthusiasm and charisma have been infectious in our community.

As the Executive Vice President of the Shenandoah Chamber and Industry Association, I felt it was important that Doug share his "secret to success" with the rest our membership. Doug not only joined the chamber of commerce, within one year he was board president. As other members talked about the problems of retail in small town America, Doug talked about the opportunities and success that was available to our small town retailers if they changed their approach towards sales and service.

A few months ago, Doug approached me about a book he was writing about how to be successful in retail in small town America. After reading the book, I was convinced this book needed to be available to every retail business in every small town in this country. To those that say small town retailers cannot compete with the internet, big box stores and big city ad blitzes, I say read this book! The small town "mom and pop" retailers of America have a champion that not only talks the talk but walks the walk.

Gregg Connell, Executive Vice President
Shenandoah Chamber and Industry Association

CONTENTS

I grew up in and around several rural towns. The first town I lived in had about 110 people. It was located in eastern Nebraska, just outside the town of Manley, which had a small country school that I attended through second grade. After that I was transferred to a bigger school in Louisville, Nebraska, which was a town of about 1,100 people. By the time I graduated from high school, I was living in Adams, Nebraska, a town of about 450 people.

When you grow up in a rural community, there is always plenty of work to do. I did everything from baling hay, walking beans, cutting hogs, and feeding cattle to working at a fast food place and a grocery store. If you want to make money, it is not a hard thing to do as long as you are willing to work. That is a lesson I learned from my father. That work ethic got me to where I am today.

From the time I was about fourteen years old, I wanted to get into the car business. My uncle was in the car business in Omaha, Nebraska. He would be driving a different car every time I saw him, and he was always doing well. Plus, I was like every other teenager. I was fascinated by cars. I was intrigued by every new option or accessory and excited about the new styles. That is what first got me interested in selling cars.

My parents thought I should try college or anything but the car business, and that is what I did for a year after high school. I went to a business school in Lincoln, Nebraska, to get a degree in computer programming. While I was attending college, I also sold computers for about thirty-five hours a week for a big box store. I learned quickly that I had a knack for selling things. I was soon leading the company in sales. At age nineteen, I got a job offer to open a new store in Texas, where I would be one of the sales managers. My uncle, however, told my father that maybe I should try selling cars. I did that instead, and I have been doing it ever since.

Now my father, mom, and brother are in the car business with me. My brother started selling cars with me in Omaha when he was twenty-one years old. I moved on to a different dealership, and I started getting different sales, finance, and leasing manager jobs. In 2003 my father decided to sell his trucking business, jump into the car business, and buy a dealership where we could all work together.

We opened our first Chevrolet dealership in Auburn, Nebraska, in 2004. Then we opened a second dealership in Shenandoah, Iowa, in 2013, and most recently a third store in Maryville, Missouri. All three stores are in small towns: Auburn has about 3,500 people, Shenandoah has around 5,500, and Maryville has a little over 12,000. Business is going well, and we love living and working in small towns.

We took everything we learned from our first dealership and our years in the car business, and we applied those principles to the second dealership we bought. Using the very same principles that are set out in this book, we increased the business at least 400 percent across the board. We started selling four times as many cars and doing four to five times as much service work. Also, our body shop business went from nearly nothing to being booked out for two weeks in advance most of the year. After stepping in to take over a dealership that was barely holding on, we turned it into the place where people wanted to do business.

At the Maryville location, we are using the same principles that we used in our first and second dealerships. Within a short time, business increased over 200 percent, and we are still growing and building that operation.

I always tell everyone, "We didn't reinvent the wheel; we just made changes to match the way people like to buy." How people purchase products has changed a lot over the past ten to fifteen years. It will continue to change.

If you don't change with people's buying practices, then you will be asking yourself this question: "Where has all my business gone, and why am I not selling to those people any longer?"

Years ago we didn't have smart phones, iPads, tablets, high speed Internet, or many of the comforts and technological advances that we do now. All of this new technology has changed the way we do business, the way we buy and sell things, and the way we live our day-to-day lives. Doesn't it make sense that business practices have had to change as well?

As I drive through the small towns in Nebraska, Iowa, and Missouri, I see businesses that are thriving and businesses that are not. I see more empty buildings in some of these small towns than I saw the previous year. I always hear the same excuses: "The economy is not what it used to be." "Everyone is buying online now." "People drive to the bigger cities more often to shop."

This book is simply everything that I have noticed about what works for selling in small towns. It is not rocket science, just basic principles for selling in a small town or rural market. My hope is that this short, quick read will help some small-town businesses—like yours—be more profitable so that they are around for my kid to enjoy.

CHAPTER 1

MOST PEOPLE WANT TO BUY LOCAL

Most people want to buy local—but you need to give them a reason to. I have heard a lot of business owners say, "They should buy from me because I have a business in town!" Those owners are right. Customers in your area *should* give you a chance. What you do with that chance is up to you.

You spend money sponsoring organizations and donating to every organization representative who walks through the door, and you wish the town would support you more in return. The key is to capitalize on every *person* who walks through the door.

It is best to treat each person who enters your store looking for a donation just the same as you would a customer. If the person is already a customer, then you should be happy that a customer is there asking you for a donation. If the person is not a customer, you should be positive—because he or she might *become* a customer.

When people visit your business, you have your chance to make a great impression from beginning to end. How you greet the customers is important, as is your process for trying to sell them your product. How the customers feel when leaving your store is also very important. If you don't want to be there or you act like their business doesn't matter to you, then the customers will know it.

Our process for communicating with visitors to our store is very simple; we teach our process to every salesperson who works for us before he or she talks to any customers. As our salespeople start interacting with customers, we review each contact the salespeople had. We review how well the salespeople stuck to the process, and we critique everything they said. After a couple of months, they know to follow the process every time because the process makes them more money and makes the customers happier.

So, what is the process? First, you have to greet your customers in an enthusiastic, positive way. Let them know from the beginning that you are excited they are there.

Next, try to build some rapport, find some common ground, and find out what they are looking for. When a customer says, "Just looking," you must be proactive.

"Great!" you should say. "What are you looking for?" You should then offer examples of the products you sell. For instance, in the car business we might say, "Great! What are you looking for—a car? A truck? An SUV? A van?"

The customer always responds with one of those vehicle choices. It is a little hard for them to say that they are "just looking" at this point. If, however, they say "I'm just looking" again, that's their signal that they need some space. Give it to them, but remain attentive.

Once you get the customer talking, it becomes a good time to talk about anything else than what you are selling in your store. What has always worked best for me is finding that common ground. (We'll explore this in greater detail in chapter 12, "Getting to Know Your Customers.") Usually with just a few questions, I can find some common ground. Perhaps this new customer is the friend of one of your existing customers. Finding that sort of common ground is huge; it makes your customers feel comfortable knowing that someone they know is already doing business with you.

After you have found some common ground, you show them your product. With automobiles, we show them all of the features on the interior and exterior of the car, the engine, and all of the new technology. *You must sell customers on what you sell in your store.*

After you have done a good job with these steps, you should ask for the sale. How you ask for the sale will be based on what you are selling. In our business, we say, "Is this something you want to try to make a deal on?" In your business, you might say, "Is this something I can get wrapped up for you?" Whatever it is, ask for the sale; *don't expect customers to just say they are going to buy it.*

Be careful that you don't come off as pushy. There is a difference between being forthright and being pushy. Customers need to know that you *want* to sell them something. It helps them to know that their business is important to you.

Once you have made the sale, don't forget also to *thank* customers for their business. You also should offer great service after the sale. Attaining both of these goals is much easier if you can capture the customers' contact information so that your business can stay in touch with them. You can send them letters in the mail or else e-mail them when you have a sale or a special event. Just try to keep in contact with them the best way you can.

When we sell cars, we get all of the contact information of customers. We stay in touch, starting with a follow-up call a few days after the purchase to make sure everything is going well. Then they receive a letter from the salesperson and a letter from me expressing thanks for doing business with our company. In three months, we send another letter to remind customers it's time for the first oil change. In six months, we send another letter to let them know we hope they still enjoy their vehicle. We also have two goals with this letter: we invite them to call with questions, and we ask for referrals. One year after their purchase, we send them another letter congratulating them on one year of owning the new vehicle.

Obviously, your ways of contacting your customers will be different if you are not in the car business. You should look for ways to keep your name in front of them at all times. You do not want them to shop somewhere else because they forgot who you are.

You also want your customers to feel comfortable in your store. The customer can pick up on everything. Many little things make the customer feel either content or uneasy. You definitely always want your customers to have a comfortable feeling.

If they are comfortable, they will stay in your store longer and spend more money. A comfortable customer enjoys the experience of being in your business and remembers that feeling when leaving. A comfortable customer comes back, buys from you again and again, and last of all, tells everyone about the comfortable experience.

An uncomfortable customer can't wait to get out of your store. An uncomfortable customer will not buy anything. That person will not come back. The uneasy, distressed customer tells his or her friends about being uncomfortable at your business.

You have to ask yourself, "What makes these customers uncomfortable?" It might be seeing your staff gossip or argue in front of customers. It might be an employee of yours who brings personal problems to work. It might be an employee who rubs everyone the wrong way. Whatever the situation is, you have to fix it—right away.

When dealing with employees, I've found great wisdom in my father's advice to ask myself a certain question: "Would I hire this person back if they quit?" If the answer is no, then it is time for you to find someone else.

There are numerous ways to make customers feel comfortable in your store and to keep these customers buying local. I will lay these methods out for you in this book. I will talk about setting the right price, having outstanding customer service, creating a professional environment, fostering a great staff attitude, and getting involved in your community. I will also talk about all the different types of advertising that work in your town.

The bottom line is that you can't expect people to buy from you simply because you have a business in town. *They are only going to buy from you if you give them a reason to buy.*

CHAPTER 2

PRICE

One of the ways to get people to buy local is competitive pricing. I truly believe that most customers *want* to support you and their community, but they will not pay hefty prices to do so. You should have competitive prices on everything you sell. You can't expect a customer to buy from you if your prices are considerably higher than the competition's.

How do you price competitively? First, shop for similar products and services at other stores around you and in nearby cities. Also, research online merchants. Once you have the facts, ask yourself what you would do if you were the customer. How much would you feel comfortable paying for that service or product?

I'm sure there are businesses you don't patronize because you think that their prices are always too high. It might be time for you to look in the mirror. Are you sure that you aren't one of *those* stores?

In my business we sell both new and used cars. On the new car side, it is pretty straightforward. A certain new vehicle with certain options will have the same manufacturer's suggested retail price (MSRP) as the exact same vehicle somewhere else. These vehicles also have the same rebates. We search the Internet within a hundred-mile radius of our dealership and make sure we have a competitive price. When a person buys a new vehicle, the person usually trades in his or her current vehicle to offset some of the new vehicle's price (a trade-in is something most businesses don't have). The difference between vehicle dealers usually comes down to the values they put on the trade-ins. The main thing is that we make sure we have a competitive price on the new vehicle so we at least get the customer to drive into our business.

On used vehicles, it's a little different. Because no two used vehicles are exactly the same, there is no direct comparison shopping to be done. The vehicles might have different miles, be in different conditions, have different options, etc. We search the Internet in the same hundred-mile radius as we do with the new vehicles. We simply look at used vehicles with similar options and mileage, and we price our used vehicles at or below the competition's price.

Our method of pricing our vehicles this way has several advantages. First, my salespeople and I can tell potential customers with absolute confidence that our prices are at or below anyone's prices within one hundred miles. Second, when people in my community look online, they can see that I'm offering fair prices upfront. This is the opposite of what they usually think regarding car dealers. Also, this creates an atmosphere of confidence for my customers and salespeople that everyone is treated fairly. Our customers understand that they don't have to go out of town to get a good price.

Even if you don't have the lowest price, most people will pay a little more to shop local. The key is figuring out how much that little amount of money is. As I said before, we are normally at or below other dealerships' prices. In some rare instances we are a little higher. In those instances we expect people to pay a few hundred dollars more for something they can buy locally from us. On a thirty-thousand-dollar vehicle, that is only 1 percent of the price. For that little extra that they pay, we will take good care of them after the sale, give them a vehicle to drive when their car is in service, and help them in any way we can.

In our town we have a very nice shoe store. This store is very active in the community and supports many organizations. I would say that on average, that store's shoes cost about five to ten dollars more per pair than at some of the big box stores in Omaha. For five or ten dollars extra, I am more than happy to buy from the store in my town so I can stay local and support a great business. Plus I can't drive to Omaha and back for five to ten dollars in gas.

Now, if the pair of shoes at the in-town store were twice as expensive or cost thirty to fifty dollars more than what I could get outside of town, then I might reconsider. Fortunately that is never the case, so I buy all of my shoes in our town.

I would say my wife and I are not that different from most customers in town. We have to watch every dollar to make things work. We don't want to spend more money than we should on the items and products we need and use in our house. We also understand the importance of buying local. We know that spending a little bit more in town will benefit numerous people, including ourselves in the long run. We just don't want to feel like we are getting taken advantage of.

One question to ask yourself is "What are some of the reasons I buy out of town?" These are the same reasons your customers are driving to the big city instead of buying from you. These people are not all that different from you.

In the next chapter I will talk about customer service. This is also something you can figure into your product's price. Great customer service is worth something; figure out what that service is worth. People don't mind paying a little more to stay within the town and have great service. But make sure you are not charging too much for the customer service.

CHAPTER 3

CUSTOMER SERVICE

Without a doubt, I know you can offer better, more personalized customer service than a big box store. That is a fact you should emphasize in your selling. Make sure that the customers know why it is better to buy from you and not somewhere else: great customer service. Tell them you can help them out with anything they need after the sale. Great customer service keeps your customers coming back to you and buying more from you.

In our business, customer service is huge. When we sell a car to someone, we make sure he or she knows to call us for anything that is needed after the sale. We offer loaner vehicles only to customers who buy from us. We offer to pick their vehicles up at their workplaces or homes to make it easier for them. We want our customers to hate the idea of buying somewhere else and losing out on all of our great customer service.

Some observers have said to me, "Maybe if you gave everyone the same service whether they bought from you or not, you would have more customers!" Perhaps, but more than likely those who typically buy from someone else would just continue to do so. And maybe my other customers would think it really doesn't matter where they buy. Many of the people who don't ever buy from us eventually wish they would have, and that is a great selling tool for us.

Just a few days ago, I received a call from a man in town who had recently bought a vehicle out of town. He reached me at my cell phone at around 8:00 p.m. He said his wife had just locked her keys in the car, and he wanted to know if I could get a key made for them. I said, "Yes, our parts department opens tomorrow at 7:30 a.m."

He asked if there was anything I could do for them that night. I asked two questions. First, where was their extra set of keys? Second, why hadn't they called OnStar? I asked the second question because I knew they should have received OnStar emergency-advisor service for free for three months, and it had not been that long since they had bought the vehicle.

He said, "The dealer we bought from didn't give me a second set of keys, and they didn't set up our OnStar."

I reminded him that if he and his wife would have bought the car in town, I would have given them a second set of keys and set up their OnStar. I also said that if all else fails, I do anything necessary to take care of my customers.

I was still nice to this individual, and I made him a key because I wanted a chance to sell him something in the future. I could have just as easily said, "Why don't you call the person you bought it from?" But if I did that, I promise you, I would never see that couple in my dealership in again.

It is amazing how fast people in the community can find you when they need special service. They somehow don't know what products you sell until they are in a predicament where they need some help. They will not go to where they bought their item, because that is too far away and they need help immediately.

I would suggest that you help these people. But also explain to them that you do sell these items and that if they plan on asking for help in town sometime, then maybe they should try to buy local. Some people won't get it, and some will. If the person gets it, then you have just picked up a new customer. As to the people who don't get it, quit doing favors for them. Save those favors for your own customers.

In every town there will be those individuals who only call you when they need a favor. They don't buy local and they never will. All of a sudden they are your best friends when they need your help, and then they forget about you after you have saved them. (The person I was talking about even had my personal cell phone number.) I help out such people once, and I tell them why they need to buy local; then I watch what happens in the following months and years. If they continue to buy out of town, then I have no problem telling them they should expect to get their special service favors out of town too. There is no requirement to give free or almost free service to someone who is never going to buy from you. But you should at least give them a chance to change.

Another way to offer great service is to give a warranty remedy on something that doesn't have a warranty on it. We sell a lot of used cars that we obtained as trade-ins. Before reselling, we have the vehicles inspected, and we fix any items we see that require repair. With used cars you can only fix what is wrong with the car at the time of inspection. It is impossible to tell the future as to which items will fail down the road. Once we have sold a used vehicle, there could be a time that a transmission or some other part goes out soon after the customer buys the vehicle. When that happens, although the vehicle was sold as-is, we might still offer to pay for some or all of the repair. The customers know we don't owe them anything, but when we do help them out, they are completely blown away by it. In most cases it wins you a customer for life.

The point is that if you go out of your way to take good care of your customer, the customer will go out of his or her way to keep buying from you. This creates a loyal customer for a lifetime.

You want your customers leaving on good terms, thinking, "Wow, I didn't expect that!" The more times you achieve that the greater number of loyal customers you will have. Such customers become loyal to you after you become loyal to them. Loyal customers will send you all of their friends and family.

CHAPTER 4

FACILITY

Here is what I want you to do. Walk outside of your business, turn around, and take a look at everything. Pretend you are looking at it for the first time. Look at your sign, your windows, your door, everything. Then walk inside and look around. Look at the floors, the corners, the ceiling, and everything in between.

Now ask yourself some questions. Does my sign describe my business? Often a business owner will pick a name that is trendy but has nothing to do with the business. Sometimes these names work and sometimes they don't. Don't be afraid to reinvent yourself and your business.

Next question. Is my place inviting? People love going to pleasant, inviting stores. When the place looks old and run down, people don't think to themselves, "This looks like a good place to get a deal!" What they do say is "I don't think I want to go in there." And they keep moving on.

I am sure you have noticed that McDonald's doesn't look the same way it did when it started, and most of its stores don't look the same way they did ten years ago. Why? Because McDonald's people know they need to change with the times. What was once a great-looking place to eat loses its appeal. McDonald's people keep reinventing the company with modern places, updated interiors, and new menu items.

When was the last time you painted or updated your place? If your answer is more than a few years, then you would be well-advised to get to work. You should constantly be doing something to update your facility. A little paint goes a long way, and it freshens things up a bit.

It is amazing the differences you will see among small-town businesses. Some always look new and fresh, and some look like they haven't changed since 1975. If your place looks like it did in 1975, then you've got a lot to do. The good news is that it doesn't take a ton of money to do a little painting and change things up a bit. But I promise it will be money that is well invested.

If you decide your place is outdated or unappealing, how do you proceed? It is much easier than what you might think. First, decide which changes you want to make. Maybe ask for some ideas from friends or other business owners who you are close to.

Next, start making those changes! You don't have to do it all at once, but you can do a little at a time. Maybe get a new sign or repaint the front of your store. Give it a fresh look. Your customers will notice for sure. More important, you will get some new customers who haven't noticed the place or don't stop by because of how it looks. I am sure you will also get a variety of good compliments.

Maybe after six months or so, start on repainting or redecorating the inside of the building. The important thing is to always be doing something to keep it looking nice. Perhaps you need new carpet, flooring, tile, drywall, an air conditioner, or something else.

Just take your time. You don't have to do it all at once. Simply keep on top of it and make some good, gradual changes. Soon your business will be looking nice and new, and your customers will like it. You will also start seeing more new customers.

The second dealership we purchased looked exactly as it did when it was built almost forty years earlier. The first thing we did was paint the outside of the building. We used more modern colors, and we put a new sign on the front of the building. Six months later we painted the whole interior of the building. We added some accent walls and hung some new pictures. Also, we made a community wall showing all of the thank you letters and commendations we received from organizations in town. And just recently we replaced a bunch of ceiling tiles to improve the appearance.

We didn't do all of these things at once, but people kept noticing the changes. Customers like to see you making updates and bettering the place at which they do business.

Last of all, make sure your place is always very clean. If you don't have the time to clean it yourself, then hire someone to do the job for you. It doesn't cost that much to keep everything clean, and it makes a world of difference.

At our business we have a lady come in and do a good, deep cleaning of our business twice a week. She sweeps in all of the corners and hard-to-reach spots, cleans all of the bathrooms, dusts the desks and chairs, removes the trash, mops the tiled areas, and vacuums the carpet.

Then, during the week on the days she is not here, we have someone touching all of these things up. Every morning the person empties the trash, cleans the bathrooms, and sweeps or vacuums any areas that need it.

There is nothing worse than a customer of yours needing to use the restroom and feeling disgusted by it. It just leaves a bad impression on the person. You don't need that when it involves something as simple as keeping a bathroom clean.

Maintaining a clean and updated facility will do more than you will ever know. It keeps your customers feeling comfortable about doing business with you. The more comfortable your customers are the more they will buy and the more referrals they will send you.

CHAPTER 5

ATTITUDE

Attitude is everything! It will make or break your business. We all have personal lives outside of our businesses or our jobs, but we can't let that get in the way of us being successful.

"Whether you're a lion or a gazelle you need to wake up running." I see so many people become complacent over time. They start their business with a great, full-speed-ahead attitude and with the goal of being the best operation in town. Then, years later, each day becomes just another day at the office for them—and it shows. You can tell they don't want to be there. They are just waiting for the day to be over. Success, however, comes from waking up with a go get 'em attitude and trying to do your best every day with a positive outlook.

We all have heard that "you only get one chance to make a good first impression." If you have ever been to any sales trainings, you know that they all will tell you that customers decide whether they like you or not within the first two minutes of meeting you. Those first two minutes are so important to selling.

Just as shown in the previous chapter, you must have the right people in place to make this happen. If you have an employee who is rude to everyone, then you will have a hard time maintaining the proper *attitude* within your business.

"The harder you try the luckier you will be!" Meet your customers with a smile. Ask them how they are doing, and ask them how you can help them. The first thing the customer is going to say 90 percent of the time is "Fine, and I am just looking."

Your quick response has to be an enthusiastic "Great, what are you looking for?"—followed by a general list of the types of things you sell. As I said before, in the car business we say, "Great, what are you looking for? … Car, truck, or SUV?" If you sold women's clothing you could say, "Tops, dresses, or pants?" The customer will have a difficult time saying "just looking" again. More likely the customer will answer with one of the items you listed.

Once you get the customers talking, ask them anything not related to that. Try to build some rapport. Ask them where they are from, how they decided to shop in your store—anything. Just make the customer feel comfortable, and have the *attitude* that you are there to help.

I have been to many small-town businesses in the place where I live, in towns in the area, and all across the United States. You can just instantly tell which businesses want to sell you something and which really don't care whether or not you are there. Unfortunately, I bet, all the owners of those businesses want me to buy something from them, but their employees don't care.

Sometimes, however, I am surprised when I get unenthusiastic service and I find out the person I interacted with was the owner.

I walked into a business where I had previously lived. I was looking for some clothes for a trip that my wife and I had planned. No one greeted me, said hi, or even acknowledged that I was there. I had to look for someone in this fairly small store to help me, and that person acted like talking to me was a waste of time. I told the salesperson that I was going on vacation to Cancun. I said I was looking for some T-shirts I could wear while at the beach or sitting by the pool. (If you could see how easily I sunburn, you would know why I needed the T-shirts.) After I explained what I wanted, the person quickly said, "Sorry, it looks like we don't carry or have in stock what you are looking for." So I left, and I felt like that store wanted me to leave.

The next business I went to was completely different. A salesperson greeted me right when I walked through the door. I told him the same story about going to Cancun and looking for T-shirts. He showed me everything the store had. He also told me that if they didn't have the right size or style in stock, he could place an order for it. I ended up ordering some things, and while I was looking around I bought some new shoes too.

All totaled, I spent about $170 in this business within about ten minutes because the salesperson had a great attitude and helped me get what I needed. What I remember the most was thinking, "This salesperson is really doing a great job, and I can tell he wants to help me out!" He had a great *attitude*!

I have been in both of these stores numerous times. The second store always sells me something when I go there. They just seem to want to every time. But at the first store, I have bought only a few items over the years. I always feel uncomfortable in their store. I get this feeling that they think I am wasting their time. The point is that every customer picks up on your *attitude*, whether it is good, bad, or an attitude of "just another boring day at the store."

A customer usually leaves a place of business carrying one of three impressions: (1) "Wow, that was a great experience!"; (2) "I don't think that employee likes that job"; or (3) "I am never going back there again." Obviously, we all want it to be the first one on the list!

CHAPTER 6

ADVERTISING

In the words of Jim Earp, the owner of the first car dealership at which I worked:

> Early to bed;
>
> Early to rise;
>
> Sell like hell,
>
> And *advertise*!

Advertising has changed so much in the last ten years. How people spend their downtime has changed, and this has affected which type of advertising works. Thankfully, in most towns, some of the old ways of advertising still bring great results. You should plan to use a few of the new methods to keep in front of the younger people coming up in your community as well as people who are visiting.

Of course, advertising comes down to four areas: print, radio, TV, and Internet. In this chapter I focus on the first three areas; the next chapter is devoted to Internet advertising.

Print

Print includes daily newspapers, among other publications. Most towns also have a "shopper" paper made up mostly of advertisements. In some cases the local newspaper owns the shopper, but sometimes the shopper will be run by a completely different company.

I prefer that the shopper papers run the majority of our ads. We have contracted with two shoppers (in Nebraska and Iowa) to run our ads on the back page every week of the year. By advertising consistently and in the same place you will have customers every week looking for your ad. Perhaps they bought from you before and want to see what you have on sale. Or maybe they have never been in before but are intrigued by your ads.

By making a long-term contract with the ad department, you should get a better rate on the ad. These newspapers are just like every other business in the way that they negotiate. It is a lot better for them to know that you will be sending the same check every month for every week that you advertise. It makes it easier for them to set up their budgets, so for this they will give you a better deal.

The other thing we like about the shoppers is that our older customers read them. Most of our older customers don't have computers, iPads, or smart phones. The only way for them to see what we have for sale is to read our shopper advertisement. Many times they will bring the shopper with them, so it is easier for them to find the car they are looking for.

Sponsorship advertising is a great way to maintain a high profile. In the local newspaper, you can usually find our business name anywhere from one to three times every week. Also, we sponsor the church directory, school events, sports teams, and special town events with signature ads. These ads are very inexpensive, usually only ten to thirty dollars per advertisement. This keeps your name in front of people and lets them know you are supporting what is important to them.

Some small towns do not have a shopper; they just have local newspapers. If that is the case, then you probably want to run a regular ad in your local newspaper. Keep your name in front of as many people as possible.

Radio

Radio is still strong in small-town America, but is fading a bit in the big cities. In the big cities, most people are listening to national radio or music on a satellite receiver or smart phones. In a small town, people still listen to that local radio station for stories about their community, events going on around town, local team scores, and happenings at the school.

It's no secret that all people, including me, like to talk about their children. What's even better is hearing on the radio about the fifty-five-yard run your son or grandson made to win the football game, or that last minute score that your daughter made that won the game. Radio is just different in a small town.

The local radio station for your town likely will have lower rates than a station in the nearest big city. Normally with local radio you can get packages that run around five to ten dollars per thirty-second spot or ten to twenty dollars per sixty-second spot.

The radio station will even help you come up with a commercial by using its deejays or a third party. You can also record the commercial yourself. It just depends on what type of audience you are going for.

At our dealerships we have done just about everything when it comes to radio advertising. We have had the deejays come up with some radio ads; we created a jingle with a third party; and I have voiced the commercials myself. Most recently my brother has been doing a radio ad with him and his two kids. In the ad that my brother and I have been running, we promote that we are a family owned and operated company. This has been great for us. In the commercial I talk about all of the roles my family plays in the day-to-day operations of the dealership. People enjoy hearing my brother's children on the radio. People love hearing that we have strong family values and work together.

The challenge with radio is that you will have a hard time really knowing how it is working for you. It is just another way to keep your name in the minds of your customers. Of course, if you see new people in your store, you can ask them where they heard of you or why they came to your business.

Television

TV is, of course, normally the most expensive, but in my market it is cheaper than radio. I advertise on the cable networks in my area. The cable company people shot a commercial for me for only $250, and they came up with a package that costs us about $6 per thirty-second spot. I did my advertising around college football and March Madness because that is big in my area. If you are at the local sports bar or at home watching a game, it will be difficult to miss my commercial.

Something to keep in mind is that in homes, people often record their favorite TV and cable shows. When it is time to watch them, the people fast-forward through the commercials. People generally do not record a sporting event, because they will see the score and highlights before they will get a chance to watch it. When viewers watch sports or other shows as they are first broadcast, viewers have little choice but to watch the commercials; at least they can't fast-forward through them. You can choose to advertise on shows most likely to be watched when they are originally broadcast.

———•———•———•———

No matter what types of advertising you do, you should look at your return on investment. You must look at the potential profit you will make from these ads and see if it makes sense. What is most important of all is to track your advertising. The radio and TV ads will be tougher to track, but if you ask some questions, it will be a little easier. Ask your customers how they heard of you. If you are running a sale, ask them, "Are you here for the sale?" If they say yes, ask them how they found out about the sale. This will help you put your advertising dollars to good use.

Next we will turn to the Internet, which provides many avenues for cost-effective advertising and promotion.

CHAPTER 7

INTERNET AND SOCIAL MEDIA

Recently I had a conversation with our Internet site's webmaster, Jeremy Vontz, who is also owner of Advanced Auto Dealers. Jeremy and I are in the group of people born between 1971 and 1981, who are now in their midthirties to midforties. Speaking of the necessity for businesses to have a web presence, Jeremy said, "If you are not online, you don't exist to people our age!"

We were the kids who started getting into computers while we were still in school. We remember the Apple II coming out in our schools. We remember when the Internet appeared. We recorded songs on cassette tapes when we were kids, then burned CDs, and now download MP3s to our flash drives or smart phones. We love technology and use it every day.

I want you to think of the businesses or attractions in your town that bring new people in every day. Think of the local hotel that is always busy or the restaurant that always has people from out of town. Now I want you to think about these people planning their trips to your town. I know this as a fact: nine out of ten of those people planned or booked their visits online.

In our town we have two big factories. These factories employ more than six hundred people between them. These companies also have factories all over the United States, so there are new people coming into our town every week. These visitors are managers and engineers who come for a week to do some work at the factories.

These people book their hotel stays online, along with their air travel and maybe even rental cars. That is not a huge shocker to anyone reading this. What you don't think about, though, is what else they look for online. They are people just like you and me, and they want to do more than just work while on their business trips. And if they are in town for shopping or dining, they want to do more than just hit that destination that brought them to town. They want to check out the local "places to be"!

If you don't have an online presence, then you are missing out on all of these visitors. These people look online regarding where they are going to eat, where they will shop for a gift for someone's birthday or special occasion, and which places they want to visit. These people look online to plan out everything about their trips.

Now, I doubt that one of these out-of-town people will buy a car while they are here, but you never know. When they Google me, they will see my website, my Google ad, our Facebook page, and more. They can also see Google reviews as well as reviews on our Facebook page. We take great pride in having favorable reviews.

Another point that my friend Jeremy made to me is that people just shop differently today. They go online and see if your store is a place they want to visit. In the past people would drive into town, park out front of your store, and walk in to check it out. Now people go online and look for your website. If your store appears to be a place they are interested in, then they will make the trip to your store.

The truth is that people are just busier now. In the United States today, we work longer hours, and our children are in more activities. We just don't have time to drive from store to store to see if you have what we are looking for. So we go online to save time.

What is necessary in order to get your business online? Chances are that the older you are the harder you think this will be. Maybe you have never done much with a computer or you have thought you don't need the Internet for your business. I've got news for you: *You are wrong!* You must have an online presence to be in today's market.

Now, don't get all overwhelmed about getting a website. It is pretty easy. First, if I were you, I would look at who has websites already in your town. Ask these people if they can tell you who designed their websites for them.

When I served as vice president on the board of our local chamber of commerce, I negotiated a deal with a web designer (my friend Jeremy) to benefit local businesses. Any business in town could get a website for a set-up fee of two hundred dollars and a monthly maintenance fee of twenty-nine dollars. Jeremy also came to a retail chamber meeting to explain how he could help the members.

Once you get a website, it is important to update it regularly. Don't just create a website, forget about it, and hope everyone will start flying in the door of your business. We have to update our inventory on our website daily. This includes removing anything that we have sold.

How people contact you from your online presence has also changed. In years past customers would visit our website or a third-party website and then call us before coming in. They would mention the particular vehicle that they saw listed. Nowadays they simply print out a map or download our address and just come in. It becomes very embarrassing very fast when you have to tell the customer, "Sorry, we sold that weeks ago!"

Then they would say, "Well then why did I just see it on your website an hour ago!"

Here are a couple of reasons to keep your website updated—including descriptions of your inventory or offerings. First, if a customer comes to your store for something the customer saw on your website and now it is not available in your store, he or she likely won't be back or visit your website again. Second, ideally you have interested shoppers looking at your site monthly, weekly, or daily. A new item might pique their interest so that they come in.

As everyone knows, Facebook has taken over the world. You would be hard pressed to find anyone who has not heard of Facebook. You can find some people who have never used it, but I guarantee you that even they have heard of it.

Facebook was originally made as a social networking website for college students so they could find out if someone was dating, in a relationship, or single. It grew into the largest social media website on the planet.

The best thing about Facebook is that it is completely free to have a Facebook page for you as a person or for a business. Plus, if you have ever been on a computer or used the Internet, you can probably figure out how to use Facebook. If you can't, find someone who can. This will be very important.

So, how do you get started? First, start a personal Facebook page for yourself. Establish an online "friend" status with everybody you know. The more friends you have on Facebook the more people you can advertise with. I have over a thousand Facebook friends. I would say less than one hundred of them are people I talk to on a regular basis. Most of them are friends from high school or past jobs I had.

Once you have done that, make a business Facebook page. Upload a cover photo and a profile photo. These photos should be relevant to your business. In the section of your page called About, describe what your business is and what your purpose is.

After you have your business page up and running, ask all of your friends to click "Like" at your page. This is another good reason to have numerous Facebook friends. Hopefully they will share with their friends and soon you will have a bunch of potential customers looking at your page.

The next step is to post on Facebook your special deals, articles related to your field, and pictures of happy customers. We take a picture of any customer who will let us—right before the person takes home his or her new vehicle. They are so excited and happy, and you can see it in the pictures. Hopefully they tag themselves, share it with their friends, and describe the great experiences they had buying vehicles from us.

When you have a Facebook page for your business, there is a section called Insights. This area shows you how all of your posts are doing. It tells you how many people you reached with each post. I have had posts that reached more than 2,500 people. Each one of these people looked at my post. Usually the most frequently read posts involve one where the customer is tagged in the picture because the Facebook user is already friends with the salesperson or me, the dealer.

The average number of people we reach in a post is probably around two hundred to three hundred people. Wouldn't it be nice if every time you sold something, the customer would let two hundred to three hundred of their friends and your friends know about it? I think so; that is why I post such news on our Facebook page.

You can also boost your posts by spending a little money with Facebook to help even more people see some of your favorite posts. You can spend as little as five dollars to have Facebook share your post with other Facebook users in your market that you are not "friends" with. When they click on your post, it will take them to your Facebook page.

Last of all, you should be careful what you post on your personal page and your business page. You don't want to show support for something that could offend many people in your customer base or post something that portrays you or your business negatively.

I use my personal Facebook page to post family events and pictures so that the rest of my family and friends can see them. I also like to post uplifting, positive videos, pictures, and quotations.

I know that there is a good chance people will do a little research about me before they do business with me. I do not want to give them any reason not to buy from me. I want them to see my Facebook page and feel good about doing business at my dealership.

CHAPTER 8

GET INVOLVED

Don't expect your community to support you if you don't support your community. Get involved, but be careful what you get involved in. Participate in activities with your church and some organizations such as the Optimist or Rotary clubs or the Elks. And be an active member of your local chamber of commerce.

Getting involved in your community will not only make you feel good for helping others, but also it will get you out there meeting all kinds of people. Believe it or not, everyone doesn't know who you are or what you sell. If you are not personally circulating in your community, then you shouldn't expect your neighbors to figure you out.

We receive donation requests for every organization, fund-raiser, and special event in town. It is great that we can donate to so many different causes. Unfortunately, people don't realize how much a business is spending on all of these donations. In our business it is thousands of dollars every year.

Sometimes, it seems, people shop for cars elsewhere but become friendly with me when they seek a donation. This pains me. Such a person might drive into our dealership in a vehicle that was clearly bought out of town. The person emerges from the vehicle and asks for one hundred dollars for his or her kid's event. I always donate, but I tell such people they might want to do business locally if they expect me to continue donating.

When you are involved in several civic organizations, you will get a return on your investment. Participating in these organizations has associated costs, but you will meet a lot more people this way. Once you get to know these people, it is going to be hard for them to buy from anyone but you. Granted, you can't sell them everything, but if you can sell them a little, that is probably more than you are currently selling them. In addition, people who associate with you in community organizations know that if they ever need your help down the road, it will be a bit awkward for them to ask you if they have never been in your business before.

I started a program in my community called Toys for Girls and Boys. I put together a plan, took it to the Elks Lodge, and asked if they could help me with it. We provide toys to less fortunate kids at Christmas. In the first year of the program, we received toys and cash donations to buy toys, resulting in more than 500 toys that were given out to 224 children in our area.

I didn't start this program to help me sell cars. I did it so that a child in my community would not wake up on Christmas morning without a toy under the tree. Of course, the families I was helping couldn't afford to buy a new car anyway.

My involvement in this program gave me a great feeling of giving at Christmas. What I never expected was how many people thanked me on a daily basis for coming up with and running such a great program for our community. My Facebook page blew up with likes and great comments. I was also mentioned several times in the newspaper and on local radio stations as someone doing some good in the community.

In my community, I am involved with the Elks, Optimist Club, and M.A.Y. Mentoring. I am on the board of the chamber of commerce. I am not at every event that all of these organizations hold, but I do get involved with quite a few of them. Most of the clubs I am in help children. The Benevolent and Protective Order of the Elks is known for helping veterans and the youth. And of course the chamber of commerce is helping the businesses in town.

We have a variety of fund-raisers and dinners at the Elks Lodge. I have participated in so many of them that I get asked to help a lot. I have pitched in frequently enough to know how to operate all of the equipment in the kitchen, including the dishwasher. So you guessed it—I get to wash a lot of dishes. I don't mind; I am just glad I can assist.

On average, I would estimate, almost every day there are a few people I don't know who say, "Hi, Doug!" On one particular day, I was out and about quite a bit. Many people who I did not recognize said hi to me, and I said hi back, just as I always do. Near the end of the day, as I had a drink with a friend, a lady was talking to me as if we had been acquainted for a while. Finally, she said, "Do you know how I know you?"

"I can't figure it out" was my reply.

"I am a teacher at the school," she said, "and I know how much you do to help children in our community. I wanted to say hi, thank you, and get to know you a little."

At that point I was proud to have helped so many children in the community and grateful that someone had noticed.

Your involvement in your community will not only help your business, but also it will make you a better person. And it will give you a great feeling to know that you helped people in your community.

The other side of the coin is not getting involved in anything political. The worst thing you can do is be on a board that makes you vote on something that will change the outcome for many people in your community.

A few examples of boards you want to stay away from are the school board, the city council, and the golf or country club board. I will give examples of each because every community has at least two of these, and most have all three.

First, the school board. Many adults in your community are worried about or at least give much thought to their children's future. All of us parents do, and we wouldn't be good parents if we didn't. The school board makes decisions that affect every child in town—and every parent of those children. As a businessperson, you don't want to be the board member who voted yes or no on a major issue that upsets half the town. If half the town is upset at you, I can promise that the people in that half will never be at your business.

Second, the city council. It is just like the school board, but now you are making decisions that affect every person in town—not just the children or the parents, but everyone. Plus, when you run for election, everyone will find out which party you support. I would say most of my customers *don't* know if I am a Democrat or a Republican, and I will not mention it here either. Why? Because I don't want the other half upset with me. How I vote and what I believe in is between me and my family, and making this public is not going to help me sell anything.

Third, the board for the golf course or country club. In every small town I have worked in there is a local golf course or country club. These places are usually owned or run by their members, who elect a board to oversee the operations of the facility and its manager. The truth is that most of these clubs struggle a little. "How do we keep membership prices down?" they ask. "How do we make the operation profitable? How do we keep the course in great condition without enough money?" If you are on the board, regardless of which way you vote or try to change things, you are in the middle of a constant struggle to survive, often a losing battle.

Plus, most of the people who care about the country club are retired people in your community. These people have a substantial influence on everything that goes on in town. They also have a lot of buying power. Most of the retirees in a small town have done well saving their money, and they can buy anything they want from anyone they want. Upsetting this group is not good for your business.

All of these boards have people who are following them and waiting for someone to do something great or make a mistake in their eyes. Either way, it is a losing proposition.

Of course we need fine people on these boards. When you retire from a great career in sales, then maybe it will be your time. Perhaps even now you can be in the background helping some of these board members with good, solid advice. You just don't want to be the person getting blamed for any decisions.

Also, with these boards I believe it is very important that you do show your support for the people on the boards. They are volunteering their time to make their community a better place to live. The least you could do is be supportive of them.

When you are asked to be on one of these boards, just say, "I can't take a chance of upsetting half the town with one decision or vote."

When I have said that, I usually have received the same response from people: "I understand you need to sell cars." They are right; that is what is most important to me.

CHAPTER 9

WHO ARE YOU AND WHO ARE YOU SELLING TO?

You have to always keep in mind who you are selling to. In the car business, it used to be that men would always wear suits and ties when selling to customers. Then we went to wearing shirt collars opened, because we found that our customers felt intimidated by the neckties. That continued for years until, at our business, we finally got rid of the suits altogether. Now we wear polo shirts in the summer, sweaters or pressed buttondown shirts in the winter, nice jeans, and dress shoes. Our female employees in the sales department also dress neatly but casually. With these slight changes in standard attire, it was amazing how much faster we broke those barriers affiliated with car salespeople.

The times had changed, and we needed to change too. Of course, we still wear suits to certain meetings, weddings, and funerals, but what we wear for business has changed since I started in the car business nineteen years ago.

Another change we have seen is the unshaven man. This is the guy who shaves about once a week and always has that three-day-growth look. While it is fine for your customers to have that look, I promise you that it will damage your chances at selling anything if your male salespeople have stubble on their faces. You want your staff to be neatly groomed and looking professional at all times. Nobody wants to buy from a slob or from people who look like they just rolled out of bed at home and went to work.

We believe that in our business we should dress a step better than our typical customer. Most of our customers are farmers and factory workers, so our wearing nice jeans, a collared shirt, and dress shoes works great for us.

The other advantage of dressing this way is that we started looking like regular Joes trying to make it in the world. With the suits, we had looked like we were trying to impress somebody, which was not the case at all. We simply had thought at the time that dressing in formal business attire was what the customers wanted from us. *We were wrong!*

The big thing you should realize in a small town is that you are usually not selling to someone with a big ego. You will find some of the best people in the world in small towns, and that is why we live and work there. Don't get me wrong, you can run into a big ego anywhere. People with big egos are in big trouble. Nobody wants to support people who think they are better than everyone else. Even if you run into people with a big ego, remember that they still like the down-to-earth guy or gal.

This leads me to my next point. Everybody's money spends the same. If your customer pays you with green American currency, a credit card, or a debit card, the money will work just the same as your own.

It is amazing to hear the countless stories about this or that place which doesn't like to sell to someone because the person doesn't have the right name or social status. I have been told the following time and time again by our customers: "We bought here because you treated us like everyone else, and you didn't care about who we were, where we came from, or where we work. You treated us fairly and wanted to sell us something."

Every time I hear that statement, I absolutely am amazed. I can't believe that a business owner or salesperson of any kind would prejudge someone based on his or her last name or where the person works. My father always said, "It doesn't matter how much money you make; it's how you spend it."

In our business, we deal with several banks that finance the vehicles people buy. We see customers whose annual incomes range from fifteen thousand dollars up to five hundred thousand dollars or more. Believe it or not, in many cases the people with the best credit are those who make just thirty thousand to fifty thousand per year. They work hard for their money and they spend it wisely. Just don't judge someone by how much money you think the person makes.

In a small town, and anywhere in the world, it is impossible to guess the people who have money. I can guarantee you that if I lined up ten people you had never met before and they were wearing their everyday clothes, you could not tell me which ones were millionaires and which were regular working people living paycheck to paycheck.

I know a guy who owns several businesses. He also owns many acres of farm ground, and day to day he farms. When you meet this guy, he usually is driving an older Chevy pickup. He is wearing jeans, a shirt that he obviously has been working in, work boots, and a ball cap. This guy has as much or more money than anyone in the town and probably the county. He is just an average, nice guy. He is not someone you would point to in a crowd while saying "That guy probably is a millionaire."

The point is that it is best for you to treat all customers fairly. Whether they pull up in a Mercedes Benz or a Kia, their money spends just the same. The biggest thing is to just acknowledge them and treat them like they belong.

Branding is also a key consideration on the topic of who you are and who you are selling to. We all think that we are selling different brands. In my business we sell new Chevrolet, Buick, GMC, and Cadillac vehicles. These are the brands that I sell. In your business you will have different brands that you sell.

What you are really selling is *you*! You are the brand. People can buy the manufacturers' brands they want anywhere, but they can't get you anywhere. It is what *you* give them that makes *you* different from anyone else.

The trick is tying you and your personal brand to what you are selling. When your community thinks of you or your name, it is best if they are focusing on you and what your business is—what you sell and can offer them.

Last of all, you should set the example that *you* do business locally too. Don't expect everyone in town to buy from you if you don't buy from your neighbors. You should be seen in town shopping and buying at other local businesses.

I support my town in any way possible. When I moved to Shenandoah a few years ago, I switched all of my life insurance and car insurance to local agents. I switched to in-town medical providers, including a doctor, a dentist, and a chiropractor. I switched all of my banking to the local bank and got my mortgage there. I do business with the companies that are locally owned and operated, such as the local drug store and gas station. I want everyone to know that I support my town's locally owned businesses. You should do the same in your town.

It's amazing how many business owners go out of town to make their own purchases. You should look for chances to educate these people on why it is important for them to do business in town.

When a business owner goes out of town to buy a product that you sell, you need to have a face-to-face talk with that person. Ask why, and explain why you buy from that person's business. What you don't want to do is act negatively toward that person or business. This will only hurt you in the long run. I myself have bought from certain local business owners who, I noticed, never bought from me. In such cases, when it is convenient and the right time, I ask them why. Sometimes they have a legitimate reason and the problem easily is solved. Sometimes they don't have a good reason. In those cases, I try to educate them on why, when they are making purchases, it is only fair to give other local business owners a chance to be the supplier. If, after all that, the person still won't do business with me, then I don't plan to go out of my way to shop at the person's business. But at least I talked to them, and I tried to make it right in a positive way.

Being negative and bad-mouthing other people and businesses will only hurt you and your business in the long run. So just try to do things in a positive way. You want to be known always as a good-natured and respectful business owner.

CHAPTER 10

HOURS OF OPERATION

T he hardest thing for me to understand in small towns is when business owners set their business hours to what works best for them, not to what works best for the customer. The last dealership we took control of had the weirdest hours. On weekdays they were open 7:30 a.m. to 5:00 p.m. for sales and service. And on Saturdays the sales department was open only from 8:00 a.m. to noon, and the service department was closed.

The first thing we did was change the hours. We added time to the end of the day because of when local people got off work. We live in a town that has two big factories. The factory workers get out somewhere between 3:30 and 5:00 p.m. every day. Before we came to town, these workers would get off work, go home, change their clothes, and come out to the dealership, only to find it was closed already. So now we are open later, and this gives customers more time to get here after they leave work.

We also created an environment in which our salespeople know that we don't leave until the last customer does. So if a customer calls and says he or she can't be here until right before closing time, then we tell the person, "No problem; we are normally here late anyway, and we are here when our customers need us to be."

We also added service hours on Saturday and kept our sales department open much longer on Saturdays. We did this for the customers who work late during the week or whose only day to do anything is Saturday.

The car business is a little different from most in the way that the inventory often can be viewed around the clock, as if the store never really closes. At our dealerships, you can drive through our lots at any time of the day or night to look at vehicles. Plus just like any business, we have a website that displays our products—in fact, every vehicle on our lot. So customers can see the inventory online at any time, and they can drive down and look at any time too.

Of course, when we made improvements, it was a challenge to some new employees or to those who had become used to doing it the same old way for many years. Some adjusted; the ones who didn't are no longer with the company. That's just the way it goes.

Expanding our availability on Saturdays was one such improvement. A service employee asked me, "Why are we open on Saturdays? No one else in town is open on Saturday."

I replied, "I think you answered your own question!"

The very first day we were open on a Saturday, a customer stopped by and thanked us for being open on Saturday. She was an elderly lady and just needed a fuse. Without us, she would have gone all weekend with that blown fuse or she might have found a new dealer to fix it for her.

I think it is common in a small town for all businesses to close around five o'clock. That is just completely crazy to me. Of course there are certain businesses that are open those hours no matter where you are at. If, however, you are a retailer who sells everyday items like clothing, gifts, and the like, then you should be open for business when people can come into your store.

It is a fact that 75 percent of all consumers spend their disposable income after 5:00 p.m. on weekdays and generally on weekends. If you are only open until 5:00 or 6:00 p.m. on weekdays, closed on Sundays, or have limited hours on Saturday, then you are missing out on a whole bunch of your town's consumers.

I would suggest that you add one hour to the end of your weekday schedule and add some hours on the weekends. Depending on which type of business you have, it might be good to be open on Sunday afternoons for a little bit. Maybe just a few hours, so people can come in and get some shopping done.

Every year around Christmas, our local chamber of commerce sends out the same e-mail to members. The e-mail can be summed up as follows: *Do we want to have our retail businesses stay open a little later this year? Do we want to start this a week or two before Christmas? And how late do we want to stay open?*

I tell them pretty much the same thing every year, but not everyone listens. It is simple. First, we want to keep everyone in town and buying local. Unfortunately, at Christmas the people are sometimes shopping for people who are difficult to buy for; they want that special gift that they don't see every day; and they have a huge list of people to buy for. Worst of all, in most cases some of these items cannot be found in town. So that makes people plan for a trip to the nearest big city for all of these items on the weekends.

What can we do to get as much of this business as possible? We can try to capture these people during the week the best we can. These people are here all week working, attending school, and living their lives. But we need to be open late enough so they can buy from us. If you are closing at the same time they get off work or not giving them enough time to run home and change, then don't expect them to be in your store. Most of these people start their Christmas shopping around Thanksgiving. The day after Thanksgiving is called Black Friday; it is the biggest shopping day of the year.

You can make your hours of operation whatever you want. Maybe you have Christmas hours, summer hours, and regular hours. It is best if you are willing to make adjustments when needed. These additional hours will increase your sales dramatically.

The biggest part of changing your hours is to commit to it. Don't just try it for a few weeks and see how it goes. When we changed our hours, it took two years for everyone in our town to notice. It is not going to happen overnight. I would also recommend that you advertise your new hours so that people know. Some of these people will give you a chance during hours that fit their schedules, while before they were not giving you a chance.

CHAPTER 11

WHEN WALMART COMES TO TOWN

If there is one thing we all know in a small town, it is that Walmart is not too far away. Many business owners look at Walmart as the death of their businesses, while others see the positives it brings to town.

I can promise you this, Walmart is doing more good for your community and your business than you think. Walmart brings people to your community from out of town; it creates more sales tax revenue in your town; it creates more jobs; and it gives another reason for people to move to your town. Once you have all of these extra people in your town, they will also shop at other stores in town. Walmart is a huge draw for the community.

As most people know, Walmart was started by Sam Walton. Sam worked at a Ben Franklin store, which had a concept similar to Walmart's. The Ben Franklin saved you five to ten cents on most items in their store, which added up to saving dollars on your bill. Sam wanted to take that idea and make it better. He went to his bosses with his idea, and they rejected it. Sam took his idea, started his own business, Walmart, and ran with it.

Walmart is now one of the biggest companies on earth. If Sam Walton were still alive, he would be one of the wealthiest in the world. Each of his heirs are among the top twenty richest people in the world.

Somewhere in the back of our minds as business owners, we each hope we can have the same success—to make one's small business into something big, something that makes substantial money for the person's family.

I just recently watched the documentary titled *Walmart: The High Cost of Low Price*. This documentary was one sided, showing all of the things the filmmakers believe is wrong with Walmart— everything from businesses closing to low wages offered to anything they could see as negative.

I will talk out of both sides of my mouth for a bit. Of course the presence of Walmart will make things tougher for businesses in town that sell any of the items that Walmart sells. I will also tell you that Walmart brings thousands of people to your town every month who may have not come in the first place.

Are there local businesses that are struggling? Of course there are. I will venture to bet they were struggling before Walmart came to town. Walmart is just a scapegoat for those business owners now.

What you should capitalize on is service and that one-on-one interaction with your customers. At Walmart you are hard pressed to find someone who knows anything about anything. They can probably tell you where the items they sell are located, but they don't know much information past that.

At your store you can be a great salesperson who knows the products you are selling. You can give the customer good information and help with any problems or questions after the sale. Good luck getting that from Walmart.

I have seen several businesses thrive in towns that have a Walmart. Some customers hate that Walmart is so big; they feel like they have to park one hundred yards from the front door, just to walk around for miles on the inside to get one thing. They would much rather park right out front of your store, walk in, get what they need, and walk out. The trick is getting those people to come to your store and to keep coming back.

If you do all of the things I have told you to do in this book, then these people will start coming into your store. Sure, they might visit your town to go to Walmart, but they might drop in at your store and give you a chance too.

CHAPTER 12

GETTING TO KNOW YOUR CUSTOMERS

When I was nearing the end of the writing of this book, I had a good friend read it. He is someone in my community who is very smart. He is about my age, a business owner, and someone who I bounce ideas off of from time to time. He said to me, "Doug, you need to elaborate on how well you know your customers, and how easy it is for you to find common ground with the new ones." We talked about this. He said I was the best he had ever seen in getting to know my customers personally. This skill, he said, made it easy for me to find common ground with my new customers. It is indeed easy because I get to know so many people through being out and about in my community. And I am involved in all kinds of community organizations.

Like most people growing up in rural areas, I experienced many small town things. In school I was in the band, and I played saxophone and drums. I also played many sports. My favorite was basketball in high school, but I also ran track and played football in junior high. For fun my brother, father, and I hunted, played golf, and did some off-road dirt biking. Also, being from a small town, I worked on farms for extra money, usually tending to crops and farm animals. I would drive tractors, ride horses, and do other tasks typical in farm life. Thus, it is especially easy for me to talk with people who have had similar experiences. But usually I can find some common ground with just about anyone.

When I meet someone, I find out what the person likes to talk about. I always take interest in what it is he or she likes to do. In many cases I have done some of the same things, so it easy to talk about that with the person. When you converse with these people about their interests, it makes them feel comfortable. It makes them feel like you're just a good ole boy or gal.

Just recently I had a customer in my office who was telling about his latest hobby, target shooting. My growing up around hunting and liking guns made it an easy conversation for me. He was telling me about all of the places he frequented. He said his favorite place was about an hour from where we live in Weeping Water, Nebraska. I asked him if he had met anyone in that neck of the woods because that is not too far from where I grew up. He said, "Yes, there is one guy who is an awesome shooter, and a really nice guy. His name is Steve." After asking a couple more questions, we figured out his last name, and he was talking about one of my best friend's father.

The point is that I got the customer talking about what he enjoyed doing—and I asked questions to find some common ground. Once we made the connection to Steve, we had even more to talk about. Sooner or later we got back to what he originally came in for, buying a vehicle. After that long conversation, he said,

"The deal sounds great; let's do it!" Maybe he would have said that anyway, or maybe he felt very comfortable with the whole situation.

When you find some common ground, people tend to think favorably of you. If the common ground involves a personal acquaintance you both know, the people think, "If my friend does business here, I might as well too." If the common ground is a hobby that you both have knowledge about, then the customer will think you are a good person to do business with because both of you like the same things. No matter what your common ground is, it makes the customers feel comfortable doing business with you.

As I said in previous chapters, there are numerous ways to meet new people and potential customers. Once you meet these people, you want them to feel comfortable buying from you. You will meet these people in a variety of circumstances: by being involved in your community's organizations; when people walk through your door in response to your new advertising; when they stop by to comment about the improvements you have made; and when you are out in the public just meeting new people. When you encounter these new people, find some common ground. Get to know them; get to know what drives them; get know what their interests are; get to know where they are from; and get to know who they know.

CHAPTER 13

CONCLUSION: GENERATING WORD OF MOUTH

Word of mouth is the best publicity and advertising that you can ever get. Word of mouth is people talking about you positively in all of the key areas I have set forth in this book. It is people talking about you generally and you as the brand.

If you put into practice the lessons of this book, people will be talking about all of the ways that you make it easy for them to buy local. They will say that you give them a good reason to buy local.

The town will start talking about your good prices that are competitive with those in the big city. The people will say that your prices are fair, which makes it easy to buy from you.

They will also say that buying from you gets them great customer service. That when they buy from you, the sale doesn't end there. That you understand that with their purchase they will receive great customer service after the sale, something they don't expect when they go anywhere else.

People in your community will talk about how you keep your facility up to date. That it doesn't look like it did ten or twenty years ago. That it is an inviting place that they enjoy going to.

They will also talk about you having a great attitude. That you are always happy, and that they enjoy doing business with you.

People in your community will start talking about all of the sales events you are having. They will talk about your advertisements that they encounter in the paper, on TV, on the radio, and on the Internet and Facebook.

Your customers will start talking about how much you are involved in the community. That you care about their town because you are making it better for them and their children. That you are there to help them when they need it.

People will say things like the following:

- "Wow, I can tell they wanted to take care of me and wanted my business!"

- "They sure do have a nice shop!"

- "Everyone I dealt with had a great attitude and was great to work with!"

- "They must always have a sale going on because I see them doing a lot of advertising."

- "I think you should give them a try. They are very involved in their community!"

- "They have great hours and are open when I can get in there!"

- "They must be doing something right; I see them all over Facebook! Lots of my Facebook friends 'like' their page."

These comments are all things you will hear if you take each of the right steps. You can't just advertise while having a bad attitude, or have a Facebook page while keeping an old-looking facility. Making it work requires doing all of the right things.

If you follow the steps in this book, I know you will be successful! Your business will start selling more. Your profits will increase. Once you experience those advances, you will have less stress and be in a better place for you and your family.

Doug Meyer started working in the car business at age nineteen in 1997, and a few years later, he convinced his brother, Brent, to enter the business. In 2004, his parents sold their trucking company to buy the family's first dealership. The family now owns several dealerships in Nebraska, Iowa, and Missouri.

For more resources to grow your business contact Selling in Your Town, LLC at info@sellinginyourtown.com